Sainsbury's

·RECIPE·LIBRARY·

BARBECUES
& PATIO MEALS

·RECIPE·LIBRARY·

BARBECUES
& PATIO MEALS

Caroline Ellwood

CONTENTS

Published exclusively for J Sainsbury plc
Stamford House Stamford Street London SE1 9LL
by Martin Books
Simon & Schuster Consumer Group
Grafton House 64 Maids Causeway
Cambridge CB5 8DD

ISBN 0 85941 471 X
First published 1986
Sixth impression 1992
© Woodhead-Faulkner (Publishers) Ltd 1986, 1992
All rights reserved
Printed and bound in Italy by Arnoldo Mondadori Editore

INTRODUCTION

The pleasure of sitting outside on a warm summer day or evening with friends, enjoying their company, good food and wine, is enormous. Barbecues and 'al fresco' meals can take place in any-sized garden or patio, or even on a large balcony.

Eating outdoors creates a relaxed and casual feel which adds to the enjoyment of the occasion. With a barbecue everyone can join in the cooking—often one finds there are too many volunteer cooks! With a little planning it can be an easy way to entertain, suitable for any time of year—so long as you are warmly dressed!

CHOOSING A BARBECUE

There are many types of barbecue on the market now, from the electric and gas operated ones to the small portable types. Take care in choosing one suitable for your needs. If you want a more permanent arrangement, build a brick one in the garden—many good DIY books give detailed instructions for this.

The all-important thing to look for when choosing a barbecue is that it is stable, capable of standing firmly on the ground when filled with charcoal and a fully laden grid. Check that screw-in or telescopic legs lock securely into position. If you intend to spit-roast, the supports should be sturdy enough to hold a large chicken or boned joint of meat.

The metal grid should be designed so that the bars are close together to prevent food dropping through onto the coals. Check, too, that the chrome-plating is of a reasonable quality.

Covered barbecues are to be recommended, as the lid acts as a reflector and cooks the food as though it were in an oven. There is much more control with this type, as the air which enters through the vents at the base of the barbecue is immediately consumed by the charcoal, causing the heat to rise up to the lid and down onto the food. This type is perfect for wet and windy days as the lid shields the food from the rain and wind. When buying a covered barbecue, check that the fire-bed is deep and has plenty of air vents, which help to control the temperature, and that the lid is close-fitting.

For small numbers of people and beginners, the hibachi barbecue is perfect; it is cheap to buy and economical to use. Choose one with a fire-bowl at least 7.5 cm (3 inches) deep.

FUEL

It is important to buy a good quality, dependable brand of charcoal. Price is a guidance here—generally the cheaper the charcoal, the poorer the quality. The success of the meal depends partly on the charcoal—it is pointless to economize on this.

Charcoal falls into two main categories: lumpwood charcoal and pressed briquettes. Lumpwood charcoal is generally made from soft wood and is inclined to burn rather quickly. When buying, check that it feels dry and light—not damp and heavy.

Charcoal briquettes are thought to give the best results, as they produce an intense and uniform heat, without sparking. They also burn for about twice as long as lumpwood, which makes them more economical to use.

Some brands of briquettes are specially treated with an ignition agent, which requires intense heat to light but means they are unlikely to go out. They burn with a red glow, rather than flaming—unless it is very windy.

LIGHTING THE FIRE

There are various ways of lighting the barbecue, and many proprietary ignition fuels on the market. In all cases, ensure that you allow enough time for the ignition fuel to burn off before cooking. This will take about 30–45 minutes, by which time most of the charcoal will be covered with grey ash. If the food is placed on the barbecue too soon it will be tainted and therefore ruined.

If you choose a liquid fire starter or gel, follow the manufacturers' instructions exactly and allow plenty of time for the fuel to burn away. A good tip is to soak a few pieces of charcoal in the liquid and leave in a glass jar with a lid, ready for the next time.

Old-fashioned solid white block firelighters are very safe, effective and cheap, but again I must stress that plenty of time should be allowed for the fuel to burn away.

A blow torch is effective and fast results can be achieved with this method, but it can be rather dangerous in the wrong hands. Arrange the charcoal in one deep layer and slowly pass the flame over it.

In daylight it is difficult to see if the charcoal is alight. *Never* put a hand near the coals to test—a good indication is a fine grey dust around the coals.

SAFETY RULES

1. Make sure that the barbecue is located away from the house, garage, garden shed, hedges and garden furniture.
2. Always keep a bucket of sand nearby in case of fire. Never pour on water, as this can damage and warp the metal.
3. Never stand matches, firelighters or other ignition fuels near the barbecue.
4. Always supervise children—do not allow them to help or investigate on their own.
5. Never use petrol, lighter fuel or any other similar volatile fuels—they are highly dangerous and impart a nasty taste to the food.
6. Never add more starter fuel to the already ignited coals—this is very dangerous. If the fire does not seem to be taking, tip the coals onto a metal tray or roasting tin and start again. The coals can be used another time.
7. Always store the barbecue in a dry place. Never put it away until the next day.

COOKING ACCESSORIES

It is not necessary to spend a great deal on accessories, but there are a few items which will be useful: a pair of long-handled tongs, a long-handled fork, a long-handled pure bristle brush for basting (a new paint brush would serve this purpose), and a server. All tools should have wooden or plastic handles. A well padded oven glove and good-size apron are also sensible, and a sprinkler bottle or plant water spray might be a good idea to dowse flames. Foil is required for some recipes: use a thick variety, or wrap the food in a double thickness of foil for best results.

THE WEATHER

Charcoal gives off carbon monoxide gas as it burns, so it is extremely dangerous to cook in a confined space or unventilated room. However, if outdoor eating is rained off, there are several possibilities.

1. Place a large sun umbrella over the barbecue and a wind shield around it if necessary. Put on wet weather clothes and grin and bear it, or take the cooked food indoors to eat.

2. Cook the food in the oven or under the grill.

3. Place the barbecue inside a fireplace with a working chimney, to draw the fumes out of the house. Make sure the room is very well ventilated. There is, of course, a risk of any smoke spoiling the decorations.

PREPARING THE FOOD

Marinating food has a dual purpose: it adds extra flavour to the food and tenderizes, meat in particular. This tenderization is due to the acid used in the marinade—that is, the lemon or lime juice, wine or vinegar. The addition of oil helps to prevent the food becoming dry during cooking.

Remove the marinating food from the refrigerator about 1 hour before cooking, to enable it to come to room temperature and develop its flavour. If this is not done, the cooking time will be affected.

Basting is very important, to prevent the food becoming dry and inedible over the intense heat. Take care not to drop oil or butter onto the hot coals, as this will cause a flare-up of flames.

NOTES

Ingredients are given in both metric and imperial measures. Use either set of quantities but not a mixture of both in any one recipe.

All spoon measurements are level:
1 tablespoon = one 15 ml spoon
1 teaspoon = one 5 ml spoon.

The alcohol measure used in the drinks section (pages 72–3) is equivalent to 2 tablespoons.

Ovens should be preheated to the temperature specified.

Freshly ground black pepper is intended where pepper is listed.

Fresh herbs are used unless otherwise stated. If unobtainable dried herbs can be substituted in cooked dishes but halve the quantities.

Eggs are standard size 3 unless otherwise stated.

Basic recipes are marked with an asterisk and given in the reference section (pages 74–9). Increase or decrease the basic quantities in proportion to obtain the amount required.

BARBECUES FOR FAMILY & FRIENDS

MENU SUGGESTION	MENU SUGGESTION
Serves 6	**Serves 4–6**
Smoked Trout and Lemon Pâté	Tandoori Chicken
Cheddar Beef Burgers	Barbecued Rosemary Lamb
Lemon Chicken	Pilau Rice
Orange and Ginger Spare Ribs	Indian-Style Courgettes
Tomato and Basil Salad	Orange and Cucumber Salad
Crunchy Bean Sprout Salad	(page 52)
Foil-Wrapped Nectarines	Barbecued Pineapple
Mulled Wine (page 73)	Honeysuckle Cup (page 72)

SEAFOOD TOMATOES

These tomatoes may also be served as the main ingredient in a salad if you double the quantities.

FOR THE FILLING:
185 g (6½ oz) can crabmeat, drained
50 g (2 oz) frozen peeled prawns, thawed
3 tablespoons Mayonnaise*
1 clove garlic, crushed
dash of Tabasco
2 spring onions, chopped
1 tablespoon each chopped coriander and thyme
1 small avocado, diced
1 tablespoon lemon juice
salt and pepper to taste
4 Marmande tomatoes
TO GARNISH:
100 g (3½ oz) jar lumpfish caviar
curly endive or frisé

Serves 4
Preparation time: 25 minutes
Freezing: Not recommended

1. Flake the crabmeat into a bowl, then stir in the prawns.
2. Mix together the mayonnaise, garlic, Tabasco, spring onions, herbs and avocado. Stir in the lemon juice and mix well. Season with salt and pepper.
3. Fold the sauce into the crab and prawns; set aside.
4. Cut a thin slice from the stalk end of each tomato. Carefully hollow out the centre with a teaspoon or grapefruit knife and discard. Turn the tomatoes upside down on kitchen paper to drain.
5. Spoon the filling into the tomatoes, piling it well above the top.
6. Arrange on a serving plate and top with the lumpfish caviar. Surround with a little curly endive. Serve chilled, as a tasty starter.

SAUSAGE PITTA PARCELS

Any of the wide choice of sausages now available can be used for this recipe. Some of the continental sausages are delicious and worth searching for.

6 large sausages	*1 small onion, sliced*
3 pitta bread	*3 tomatoes, sliced*
6 lettuce leaves, shredded	*1 quantity Tomato Sauce**

Serves 6
Preparation time:
10 minutes, plus
making sauce
Cooking time:
20 minutes
Freezing:
Not recommended

1. Prick the sausages and cook on the metal grid for 20 minutes, turning occasionally.
2. Place the pitta bread on the cooler part of the barbecue for a few minutes to warm. Cut them in half and loosen the inside of each half to make a pocket.
3. Place the shredded lettuce, onion and tomato in the pitta bread, place a sausage in each half and spoon over the sauce. Serve immediately.

FRANKFURTER RINGS

Frankfurters are quick to prepare on a barbecue, as they are already cooked prior to purchase. This recipe is perfect for hungry children to eat while the rest of the food is cooking.

425 g (15 oz) can	*6 lettuce leaves*
frankfurters, drained	*1 small onion, sliced*
6 slices matured Cheddar	*3 tomatoes, sliced*
cheese	*2.5 cm (1 inch) piece*
6 sesame seed baps, halved	*cucumber, sliced*

Serves 6
Preparation time:
10–15 minutes
Cooking time:
10 minutes
Freezing:
Not recommended

1. Make small incisions in one side of each frankfurter, then curl in pairs to form circles; secure with a cocktail stick.
2. Place the frankfurter rings on the metal grid and cook for 5 minutes on each side.
3. Move the frankfurters to the cooler side of the barbecue and top each one with a slice of cheese.
4. Place the baps, cut side down, on the metal grid and toast for 1–2 minutes.
5. Arrange the salad ingredients on the base of the baps, top with the cheesy frankfurters, then cover with the lids. Serve immediately, with Tomato Sauce* or a selection of tasty relishes.

CHICKEN AND SAUSAGE KEBABS

Use wooden skewers for these kebabs. Once used, they can be thrown away.

*250 g (8 oz) boneless
chicken breast*
*12 rashers streaky bacon,
derinded*
*500 g (1 lb) cocktail
sausages*
16 bay leaves

FOR THE BASTING SAUCE:
2 teaspoons tomato purée
*2 teaspoons Worcestershire
sauce*
*1 teaspoon French
mustard*
2 tablespoons oil
pinch of dried mixed herbs
salt and pepper to taste

Serves 8
Preparation time:
15 minutes
Cooking time:
15–20 minutes
Freezing:
Not recommended

1. Cut the chicken into 2.5 cm (1 inch) pieces.
2. Stretch the bacon on a board with the back of a knife, then cut in half.
3. Roll the bacon around the pieces of chicken.
4. Thread the chicken, sausages and bay leaves alternately onto 8 skewers.
5. Mix all the basting ingredients together and brush over the kebabs.
6. Place the kebabs on the metal grid and cook for 7–10 minutes each side, basting and turning them frequently. Serve immediately.

CHEDDAR BEEF BURGERS

The best homemade burgers are made with rump or chuck steak; it is well worth mincing it yourself, just before it is required.

*1 kg (2 lb) piece rump or
chuck steak, minced
finely*
*1 onion, chopped very
finely, or minced with
the meat*
*few drops Worcestershire
sauce*
*1 teaspoon dried mixed
herbs*
*1 tablespoon chopped
thyme*

*1–2 teaspoons French
mustard*
*175 g (6 oz) matured
Cheddar cheese, grated
finely*
*6 slices matured Cheddar
cheese*
*6 sesame seed baps, halved
(optional)*
1 bunch watercress
*250 g (8 oz) cherry
tomatoes, sliced*
salt and pepper to taste

1. Season the meat well with salt and pepper. Stir in the onion, Worcestershire sauce, herbs and mustard, then stir in the grated cheese.

2. Divide the mixture into 6 pieces and form each into a ball. Flatten slightly into a burger shape.

3. Place the burgers on the metal grid and cook for 5–7 minutes on each side, according to taste.

4. Move the burgers to the side of the barbecue and top with the cheese slices.

5. Toast the cut sides of the baps, if using.

6. Either arrange the watercress, burgers and tomatoes on each bap base, then replace the bap lids, or arrange the watercress and tomatoes on a serving plate with the cheese burgers.

Serves 6
Preparation time:
15–20 minutes
Cooking time:
10–15 minutes
Freezing:
May be frozen
before cooking

BARBECUED ROSEMARY LAMB

It is possible to buy unstuffed, boned and rolled leg of lamb—by cooking it in this way it is very easy to carve.

1 boned leg of lamb,
weighing 1.25 kg
(2½ lb)

1 quantity Cider
Marinade*
small bunch rosemary

Serves 6
Preparation time:
10 minutes, plus
making marinade
and marinating
Cooking time:
20–30 minutes
Freezing:
Not recommended

1. Lay the lamb flat on a board, skin side down. Cut it through its thickest parts, without piercing the skin, and pull apart gently. This should make the meat of equal thickness and ensure even cooking.
2. Place in a roasting tin, pour over the marinade and turn the meat over so that it is well coated. Cover and chill overnight, or for 8 hours, turning occasionally.
3. Place the rosemary on the hot coals.
4. Place the lamb on the metal grid and cook for 10–15 minutes on each side, basting frequently with the marinade, until the meat is tender and cooked to your liking.
5. Cut into thick slices and serve immediately.

BARBECUED LAMB CUTLETS

These lamb cutlets are cooked in a pan over the coals. The advantage of choosing this recipe for a barbecue is that if it is rained off you can cook indoors!

8 lamb cutlets	*2 small shallots, chopped*
1 quantity Wine	*very finely*
Marinade*, excluding	*142 ml (5 fl oz) carton*
olive oil	*double cream*
25 g (1 oz) butter	*1 tablespoon chopped*
	parsley

1. Add the lamb to the marinade, turning to coat the cutlets. Cover and chill for 4 hours, turning occasionally.

2. Melt the butter in a heavy-based frying pan, add the cutlets and brown quickly on both sides. Add the shallots and cook for 5 minutes. Increase the heat, strain the marinade into the pan, and cook rapidly for 10 minutes, turning the cutlets occasionally, until the liquid has reduced to a few tablespoons.

3. Pour in the cream and boil rapidly for 2 minutes, stirring; sprinkle in the parsley.

4. Serve immediately, spooning the sauce over the cutlets.

Serves 4 or 8
Preparation time: 10 minutes, plus making marinade and marinating
Cooking time: About 20 minutes
Freezing: Not recommended

LEMON CHICKEN

4 boneless chicken breasts,
  skinned
1 quantity Lemon
  Marinade*

TO GARNISH:
lemon slices
thyme sprigs

Serves 4
Preparation time:
10 minutes, plus
making marinade
and marinating
Cooking time:
20 minutes
Freezing:
Not recommended

1. Make 3 diagonal cuts in each of the chicken pieces. Place in a bowl, add the marinade, cover and chill for 6 hours, turning the chicken occasionally.
2. Lift the chicken pieces from the marinade and place each on a large piece of foil. Spoon over the marinade. Turn the edges of the foil in towards the centre and secure tightly to ensure that none of the juices escape during cooking.
3. Place the foil parcels on the metal grid and cook for 10 minutes. Turn the parcels over and cook for a further 10 minutes, until the chicken is tender.
4. Open the parcels, place the chicken on a warmed serving plate, spoon over a little of the juices and garnish with lemon slices and thyme. Alternatively, serve in the foil parcels. Serve with Tomato and Basil Salad (page 28).

HONEY-GLAZED DRUMSTICKS

8 chicken drumsticks
FOR THE GLAZE:
3 tablespoons clear honey
1 tablespoon
  Worcestershire sauce
1 clove garlic, crushed
2.5 cm (1 inch) piece fresh
  root ginger, crushed
dash of Tabasco

1 tablespoon mango
  chutney
grated rind and juice of
  1/2 orange
1/4 teaspoon hot curry
  powder
TO GARNISH:
orange segments
parsley sprigs

Serves 4 or 8
Preparation time:
15 minutes, plus
marinating
Cooking time:
20 minutes
Freezing:
Not recommended

1. Mix together the glaze ingredients in a bowl; if the mango chutney has pieces in it, chop these very finely.
2. Using a sharp knife, make 2 incisions in each side of each drumstick.
3. Place the chicken in a single layer in a flat dish. Spoon over the glaze, turn the drumsticks over to coat well, cover and chill for 3 hours, turning occasionally.
4. Place the drumsticks on the metal grid and cook for 20 minutes, turning frequently and basting constantly with the glaze, until cooked through.
5. Garnish with orange segments and parsley to serve.

TANDOORI CHICKEN

The success of this succulent chicken dish is very dependent on the freshness of the spices. It is well worth buying new ones, if you are in doubt.

1 teaspoon hot chilli powder
1 teaspoon ground coriander
1 teaspoon ground cumin
2–3 cloves garlic, crushed
2.5 cm (1 inch) piece fresh root ginger, crushed
175 ml (6 fl oz) natural yogurt
1 tablespoon chopped coriander
1/4 teaspoon salt
2 tablespoons lemon juice
1/4 teaspoon grated lemon rind
4 boneless chicken breasts, skinned
TO GARNISH:
lemon wedges
coriander leaves

Serves 4
Preparation time: 15 minutes, plus marinating
Cooking time: About 20–25 minutes
Freezing: Not recommended

1. Put the spices in a large bowl, add the garlic and ginger, then stir in the yogurt, chopped coriander, salt, lemon juice and rind.
2. Cut 3 diagonal slashes in each chicken breast, add to the bowl and spoon over the marinade, ensuring that they are well coated. Cover and chill for 6 hours, turning occasionally.
3. Lift the chicken from the marinade and place each piece on a piece of foil large enough to enclose it completely. Fold securely into a parcel.
4. Place on the metal grid and cook for 10–12 minutes. Turn the parcels over and cook for a further 10 minutes.
5. Open the parcels, lift the chicken onto a warmed serving plate, garnish with lemon wedges and coriander and serve immediately.

ORANGE AND GINGER SPARE RIBS

Allow time for partially cooking the spare ribs in the oven and marinating—then they only take 15–20 minutes on the barbecue. The tangy sauce imparts a delicious flavour. Serve any remaining sauce with the cooked ribs.

1 kg (2 lb) pork spare ribs
1 quantity Orange and Ginger Sauce*
several bay leaves
TO GARNISH:
orange slices
bay leaves
sliced stem ginger

1. Place the spare ribs in a roasting tin, cover with foil and cook in a preheated oven, 200°C/400°F/Gas Mark 6, for 35 minutes, until tender.

2. Pour off any fat and juices from the pan and leave the meat to cool.

3. Spoon the sauce over the spare ribs, cover and leave to marinate for 2 hours, turning occasionally.

4. Place the bay leaves on the coals of the barbecue and the spare ribs on the metal grid. Cook for 15–20 minutes, turning occasionally and basting with the sauce.

5. Arrange on a warmed serving dish and garnish with orange slices, bay leaves and ginger to serve.

Serves 4–6
Preparation time: 40 minutes, plus making marinade and marinating
Cooking time: 15–20 minutes
Freezing: Not recommended

COCONUT FISH STEAK PARCELS

*4 cod steaks, each
    weighing 175 g (6 oz)
1 quantity Coconut
    Marinade**

*2 tablespoons chopped
    coriander
TO GARNISH:
coriander leaves
lime wedges or slices*

Serves 4
Preparation time:
20 minutes, plus
making marinade
and marinating
Cooking time:
15 minutes
Freezing:
Not recommended

1. Place the cod steaks in a single layer in a shallow dish. Spoon over the marinade, then turn them over to coat the other side. Cover and chill for 1 hour.
2. Lift the fish from the marinade and place each one on a piece of foil large enough to enclose the fish and marinade. Spoon the marinade over and sprinkle with the coriander.
3. Wrap the foil around the fish and form into a parcel, sealing all the edges to ensure that it does not leak during cooking.
4. Place the parcels on the metal grid and cook for 10 minutes, then turn them over and cook for 5 minutes.
5. Remove the fish from the foil, garnish with coriander and lime and serve immediately, with jacket potatoes and a green salad.

VEGETABLE KEBABS

*3 courgettes, cut into
  1.5 cm (¾ inch) pieces
2 each red and green
  peppers, cored, seeded
  and cut into 1.5 cm
  (¾ inch) pieces
3 small onions, quartered*

*12 button mushrooms
12 small tomatoes
12 bay leaves
1 quantity Barbecue
  Marinade*
TO SERVE:
1 quantity Saté Sauce**

1. Blanch the courgettes in boiling salted water for 30 seconds, drain and cool under running cold water; drain again.
2. Thread the vegetables and bay leaves alternately on 12 kebab skewers.
3. Place in a large roasting tin and spoon over the marinade. Turn the kebabs to ensure that all the vegetables are coated and leave to stand for 1 hour.
4. Place the kebabs on the metal grid and cook for 10 minutes, turning frequently and basting constantly with the marinade.
5. Serve immediately with the saté sauce.

Serves 6
Preparation time: 20 minutes, plus making marinade and sauce, and marinating
Cooking time: 10 minutes
Freezing: Not recommended

STUFFED TOMATOES

These can be served as a starter, or vegetarian main dish; serve two tomatoes per person for a main course, one for a starter. For non vegetarians, you may add 125 g (4 oz) prawns to the filling.

8 Marmande tomatoes
FOR THE FILLING:
50 g (2 oz) butter
2 tablespoons olive oil
4 shallots, chopped finely
2 cloves garlic, crushed
50 g (2 oz) pine nuts
6 saffron threads
2 tablespoons boiling water
600 ml (1 pint) dry white wine

125 g (4 oz) Italian risotto rice
1 bouquet garni, to include bay leaf, parsley, thyme and rosemary
50 g (2 oz) button mushrooms, diced
2 tablespoons chopped parsley
salt and pepper to taste
TO GARNISH:
cucumber slices
fresh herbs

Serves 4 or 8
Preparation time:
35 minutes
Cooking time:
20–25 minutes
Freezing:
Not recommended

1. Slice the top from each tomato and reserve. Carefully scoop out the pulp and seeds from the tomatoes and reserve.
2. Heat the butter and oil in a large pan, add the shallots and cook for 10 minutes, until pale brown, stirring constantly.
3. Add the garlic and pine nuts and cook for 2 minutes.
4. Place the saffron in a small bowl, pour over the boiling water and leave to stand for 2 minutes.
5. Reserve 4 tablespoons wine. Stir the rest into the pan with the rice and add the bouquet garni. Bring to the boil.
6. Stir in the saffron and its liquid, season well with salt, cover and simmer for 10 minutes, stirring occasionally.
7. Stir in the mushrooms, parsley, tomato pulp and pepper, then cook for 5–10 minutes, until the rice is tender and the liquid absorbed. Remove the bouquet garni.
8. Spoon the rice into the tomatoes, pressing down well. Top with the tomato lid.
9. Place the tomatoes on a double thickness of foil, large enough to hold all of them and to form into a parcel. Spoon the reserved wine over the tomatoes, then fold the foil into a parcel.
10. Place the foil parcel on the metal grid and cook for 20–25 minutes, until the tomatoes are soft.
11. Serve hot or cold, garnished with cucumber and herbs.

CRUNCHY BEAN SPROUT SALAD

This salad has an oriental flavour which is perfect with barbecued meats. Any crunchy vegetables may be added to make it more substantial.

227 g (8 oz) can
  waterchestnuts, drained
  and sliced thinly
125 g (4 oz) bean sprouts
125 g (4 oz) cherry
  tomatoes
¼ head Chinese leaf,
  shredded
6 radishes, sliced

1 each small red and green
  pepper, cored, seeded
  and sliced
2 green celery sticks, sliced
2 tablespoons sesame
  seeds, toasted
6 tablespoons Soy Sauce
  Dressing*

1. Mix the salad ingredients together in a large bowl.
2. Pour over the dressing just before serving and toss well. Serve immediately.

Serves 4–6
Preparation time:
20 minutes, plus
making dressing
Freezing:
Not recommended

PIQUANT ARTICHOKE SALAD

The creamy texture and delicate flavour of fromage frais
make it an excellent base for a blue cheese dressing.

*250 g (8 oz) fresh
   asparagus
2 × 400 g (14 oz) cans
   artichoke hearts,
   drained and sliced
2 bunches watercress*

*2 heads radicchio
1 quantity Blue Cheese
   Dressing*
2 tablespoons toasted
   sunflower seeds*

Serves 8
Preparation time:
20 minutes, plus
making dressing
Freezing:
Not recommended

1. Cut the asparagus into 5 cm (2 inch) lengths, discarding
the woody ends. Cook in boiling water for 5 minutes, until
just tender. Drain well, then place in a large bowl. Add the
artichoke hearts and watercress.
2. Break the radicchio into leaves and add to the bowl.
3. Carefully fold in the dressing, then transfer to a serving
dish.
4. Sprinkle the sunflower seeds over the salad and serve
immediately.

CAULIFLOWER AND ALMOND SALAD

*250 g (8 oz) shelled broad
  beans
1 small cauliflower,
  broken into florets
1 canned pimento,
  drained and chopped
12 pitted green olives,
  halved
2 spring onions, chopped
FOR THE DRESSING:
3 tablespoons
  Mayonnaise**

*2 teaspoons grated lemon
  rind
2 teaspoons lemon juice
1 tablespoon ground
  almonds
pinch of cayenne pepper
salt to taste
TO SERVE:
25 g (1 oz) flaked
  almonds, toasted*

1. Blanch the beans in boiling water for 2 minutes, drain and cool under running water; drain and remove skins.
2. Place the beans and remaining salad ingredients in a large bowl.
3. Mix together the dressing ingredients until smooth. Fold into the salad ingredients, coating well.
4. Transfer to a serving dish, sprinkle with the almonds and serve immediately.

Serves 6
Preparation time:
15 minutes
Freezing:
Not recommended

TOMATO AND BASIL SALAD

500 g (1 lb) Marmande tomatoes, sliced thinly
small bunch basil, chopped roughly
25 g (1 oz) pine nuts

1 tablespoon coarse-grain mustard
6 tablespoons French Dressing*

Serves 6
Preparation time:
15 minutes, plus
making dressing
and marinating
Freezing:
Not recommended

1. Arrange the tomatoes and basil on a plate. Sprinkle with the pine nuts.
2. Add the mustard to the dressing and shake well to blend. Spoon over the salad, cover and leave to stand for at least 20 minutes.
3. Serve lightly chilled.

BROWN RICE AND BEAN SALAD

A fairly substantial salad – suitable to serve as a light vegetarian lunch.

250 g (8 oz) brown rice
213 g (7½ oz) can red kidney beans, drained
410 g (14½ oz) can flageolets, drained
25 g (1 oz) butter
2 shallots, chopped finely
3 spring onions, chopped
2 celery sticks, chopped
50 g (2 oz) button mushrooms, sliced

1 each small red and green pepper, cored, seeded and sliced
2 tablespoons chopped marjoram
1 quantity French Dressing*
salt and pepper to taste
50 g (2 oz) roasted peanuts, to serve

Serves 6–8
Preparation time:
25–30 minutes,
plus making
dressing
Cooking time:
30 minutes
Freezing:
Not recommended

1. Rinse the rice and beans separately under running cold water; drain well.
2. Melt the butter in a pan, add the shallots and cook gently for 5 minutes, stirring occasionally. Add the rice and stir well.
3. Cover with boiling water, add 1 teaspoon salt, cover and simmer for 25–30 minutes, until just tender. Drain well and cool under running cold water; drain again.
4. Place in a large bowl and add the beans, spring onions, celery, mushrooms, peppers, and salt and pepper. Mix well.
5. Add the marjoram to the dressing and shake well to blend. Pour over the salad and toss well.
6. Spoon into a serving dish and sprinkle with the nuts.

AVOCADO AND MUSHROOM SALAD

1 bunch watercress
2 ripe avocados, sliced
    lengthways
250 g (8 oz) button
    mushrooms, sliced

250 g (8 oz) peeled prawns
125 ml (4 fl oz) Herb and
    Peppercorn Dressing*
parsley sprigs to garnish

Serves 6
Preparation time:
15 minutes,
plus making
dressing
Freezing:
Not recommended

1. Arrange the watercress and avocado around the edge of a large flat plate and pile the mushrooms in the centre.
2. Sprinkle the prawns over the salad and spoon over the dressing. Serve immediately, garnished with parsley.

PILAU RICE

2 tablespoons oil	2 cloves garlic, crushed
4 shallots, chopped	250 g (8 oz) basmati rice
1 teaspoon each ground cumin and coriander	600 ml (1 pint) homemade chicken or veal stock
1/2 teaspoon chilli powder	50 g (2 oz) cashew nuts, roasted
6 cardamom pods	salt to taste
2.5 cm (1 inch) piece cinnamon stick	coriander leaves to garnish
1 blade mace	

Serves 6–8
Preparation time:
10 minutes
Cooking time:
35 minutes
Freezing:
Not recommended

1. Heat the oil in a large pan, add the shallots and cook for 10 minutes, stirring, without browning.
2. Stir in the spices and cook for 5 minutes, ensuring that they do not burn.
3. Add the garlic and rice and cook for 5 minutes, stirring constantly.
4. Pour in the stock, season with salt, cover and simmer for 15 minutes, until the rice is tender and the stock has been absorbed, stirring occasionally.
5. Transfer to a warmed serving dish, sprinkle with the cashew nuts and garnish with coriander.

INDIAN-STYLE COURGETTES

This vegetable dish has a piquant flavour and is delicious served with all barbecued food, particularly steak and chops. The courgettes should be firm, so be sure to test them halfway through their cooking time.

1 tablespoon oil
2 large shallots, chopped
397 g (14 oz) can chopped
*   tomatoes*
2 cloves garlic, crushed

2.5 cm (1 inch) piece fresh
*   root ginger, crushed*
1/2 teaspoon chilli powder
3–4 courgettes, sliced
salt and pepper to taste
parsley sprigs to garnish

1. Heat the oil in a saucepan, add the shallots and cook for 5 minutes, without browning, stirring occasionally.
2. Add the tomatoes, garlic, ginger and chilli powder. Bring to the boil, then simmer for 20 minutes, uncovered, until thickened.
3. Stir in the courgettes, season with salt and pepper, and cook for 5 minutes, until the courgettes are just tender. Serve hot or cold, garnished with parsley.

Serves 4–6
Preparation time:
5–10 minutes
Cooking time:
30 minutes
Freezing:
Recommended

COWBOY BAKED BEANS

Baked beans are always popular, especially with children.
This dish has a slightly sweet and sour flavour and is good
with sausages, burgers, chops and steaks.

25 g (1 oz) butter
1 large onion, chopped
   finely
1 clove garlic (optional),
   crushed
2.5 cm (1 inch) piece fresh
   root ginger, crushed
1 each green and red
   pepper, cored, seeded
   and chopped

2 carrots, diced
2 tablespoons vinegar
4 tablespoons clear honey
1 teaspoon Worcestershire
   sauce
2 × 450 g (1 lb) cans
   baked beans
125 g (4 oz) streaky bacon,
   derinded and chopped

Serves 6–8
Preparation time:
15 minutes
Cooking time:
20 minutes
Freezing:
Not recommended

1. Melt the butter in a pan, add the onion and cook for 10
minutes, without browning.
2. Stir in the garlic (if using), ginger, peppers and carrots
and cook for 2 minutes.
3. Add the vinegar and honey, lower the heat and cook for
3–4 minutes, stirring constantly.
4. Add the Worcestershire sauce and baked beans and stir
well. Cook gently for 5 minutes, stirring occasionally.
5. Fry the bacon in its own fat until crisp and brown. Drain
on kitchen paper.
6. Spoon the baked beans into a warmed serving dish,
sprinkle with the bacon and serve immediately.

JACKET POTATOES

Potatoes cooked in this way are always popular – they are
delicious simply filled with butter, but try one of these
fillings for a change. Each filling is a sufficient quantity for
6 potatoes.

6 large potatoes
BOURSIN CHEESE
   FILLING:
2 × 142 g (5 oz) packets
   Boursin cheese with
   garlic
4 tablespoons double
   cream
1–2 cloves garlic, crushed

2 tablespoons each
   chopped parsley and
   thyme
2 tablespoons chopped
   marjoram or oregano
salt and pepper to taste
oregano or parsley sprigs
   to garnish

PRAWN AND CHEESE
  FILLING:
200 g (8 oz) packet
  creamery full fat soft
  cheese
1–2 cloves garlic
125 g (4 oz) peeled
  prawns
2 teaspoons lemon juice
2 anchovies, chopped finely
2 spring onions, chopped
pepper to taste

SOURED CREAM FILLING:
284 ml (10 fl oz) carton
  soured cream
1/2 teaspoon chilli powder
3 tablespoons snipped
  chives
1 tablespoon chopped dill
2 tablespoons capers
salt and pepper to taste
dill or chervil sprigs to
  garnish

1. To make the fillings, mix together the ingredients in a bowl, cover with clingfilm and chill until required.
2. Prick the potatoes and brush with oil. Place in a pre-heated oven, 200°C/400°F/Gas Mark 6, for 50 minutes, until nearly cooked. Then, if you wish, place in the hot charcoal for 15 minutes, or until cooked, turning occasionally with tongs. Alternatively, leave in the oven until cooked.
3. Serve with the chosen filling, garnished to taste.

Serves 6
Preparation time:
10–15 minutes
Cooking time:
1 hour and
5 minutes
Freezing:
Not recommended

BARBECUED PINEAPPLE

*finely grated rind and
juice of 1 orange
2 tablespoons kirsch or
Cointreau*

*1–2 tablespoons icing
sugar
1 pineapple, peeled and
cut into chunks*

Serves 6
Preparation time:
15 minutes, plus
chilling
Cooking time:
20 minutes
Freezing:
Not recommended

1. Mix together the orange rind and juice, liqueur and sugar. Stir in the pineapple and mix well.
2. Cover with clingfilm and chill for 1–4 hours, stirring occasionally.
3. Spoon the pineapple mixture onto a large piece of thick foil. Turn in the edges and seal into a parcel, ensuring that there are no gaps for the liquid to escape.
4. Place on the metal grid and cook for 10 minutes, then turn the parcel over and cook for a further 10 minutes.
5. Open the parcel and transfer the fruit to individual serving dishes. Serve warm.

FOIL-WRAPPED NECTARINES

If nectarines are not available, fresh peaches are equally good for this recipe. The rum butter is also delicious with bananas; the cooking time will be the same.

*6 large ripe nectarines
25 g (1 oz) pistachio nuts,
blanched and chopped
FOR THE RUM BUTTER:
75 g (3 oz) unsalted butter,
softened*

*40 g (1½ oz) light brown
soft sugar
finely grated rind of
1 orange
1 tablespoon dark rum*

Serves 6
Preparation time:
10–15 minutes
Cooking time:
15 minutes
Freezing:
Not recommended

1. To make the rum butter, cream the butter until soft, beat in the sugar and orange rind, then stir in the rum.
2. Place a piece of foil, large enough to accommodate all the fruit and butter, on the worktop. Spread the butter over the centre of the foil. Halve the nectarines, stone and cut into slices, then reassemble the nectarine halves on the foil. Fold in the edges of the foil to make a secure parcel, making sure there are no gaps where the butter can escape during cooking.
3. Place the parcel on the metal grid and cook for 10 minutes. Turn the parcel over and cook for 5 minutes.
4. Open the parcel, transfer the fruit and juice to warmed serving plates and sprinkle with the pistachios. Serve warm, with whipped cream.

BANANAS WITH FUDGE SAUCE

*170 g (6 oz) can
   evaporated milk
50 g (2 oz) unsalted butter
75 g (3 oz) light brown soft
   sugar*

*25 g (1 oz) plain cooking
   chocolate, chopped
6 slightly under-ripe
   bananas*

Serves 6
Preparation time:
5 minutes
Cooking time:
5 minutes
Freezing:
Not recommended

1. First make the sauce. Place the evaporated milk, butter and sugar in a small saucepan. Heat gently until the butter has melted and the sugar has dissolved, then bring to the boil and boil for 2 minutes. Remove from the heat, stir in the chocolate and mix well. Keep warm.
2. Place the bananas in their skins in the charcoal embers, just away from the hottest part of the coals. Cook for 2–3 minutes, then turn over with tongs and cook for a further 2 minutes, until the skins are charred.
3. Remove from the coals with tongs and serve immediately, peeled, with the warm sauce.

ORANGE AND LEMON ICE CREAM

Homemade ice cream is delicious, but sometimes it is a rather time-consuming job. This recipe is designed especially for ease and speed, as there is no stirring or beating once it has gone into the freezer.

*170 g (6 oz) can
   evaporated milk, chilled
   overnight
284 ml (10 fl oz) carton
   non-dairy cream
50 g (2 oz) icing sugar*

*grated rind of 3 large
   oranges
juice of 2 large oranges
grated rind and juice of
   2 large lemons*

Serves 6–8
Preparation time:
20 minutes, plus
freezing
Freezing:
Recommended for
up to 3 months

1. Place the evaporated milk in a large mixing bowl and whisk with an electric mixer until it has trebled in bulk.
2. Gradually whisk in the cream and continue whisking until it is very thick and has trebled again.
3. Whisk in the sugar and the fruit rinds and juice.
4. Spoon into a rigid freezerproof container, cover, seal and freeze overnight.
5. Remove from the freezer 15–20 minutes before required, to soften slightly. Spoon into individual dishes and serve with fresh fruit and crisp biscuits.

TOASTED MARSHMALLOWS

Illustrated top right: Ice Cream and Fruit Soda (page 72)

*2 packets pink and white
    marshmallows*

1. Place one marshmallow at a time on a kebab or wooden skewer.
2. Hold over the barbecue, turning occasionally, until golden brown and puffed up.
3. Serve immediately.

Serves 6
Cooking time:
About 1 minute
Freezing:
Not recommended

SPECIAL OCCASION BARBECUES

MENU SUGGESTION

Serves 6

Crudités with Caribbean Dip
Barbecued T-Bone Steaks
Sausage and Chicken Kebabs
Avocado and Watercress Salad
Endive and Roquefort Salad
Potato and Chive Salad
Redcurrant and Kiwi Pavlovas
Honeysuckle Cup (page 72)

MENU SUGGESTION

Serves 6

Marinated Fresh Goat's Cheese
Sardines with Lemon Balm Butter
Chicken Saté
Salad with Almond Dressing
Ratatouille with Coriander
Summer Fruit Compote
Strawberry Champagne Punch
(page 72)

CRUDITÉS WITH CARIBBEAN DIP

Use a selection of colourful fruits and vegetables for the crudités; some suggestions are given here – you might try pieces of carrot and celery, sliced bananas or grapes.

FOR THE DIP:
125 g (4 oz) creamed coconut
120 ml (4 fl oz) water
½ teaspoon each chilli powder, ground cumin and ground coriander
1–2 cloves garlic, crushed
3 tablespoons crunchy peanut butter
2 spring onions, chopped

1 tablespoon light soy sauce
salt and pepper to taste
FOR THE CRUDITÉS:
½ fresh pineapple, skin and core removed
1 slice watermelon, weighing 250 g (8 oz)
1 each red and green pepper, cored, seeded and sliced lengthways

Serves 4–6
Preparation time:
30 minutes
Cooking time:
About 7 minutes
Freezing:
Not recommended

1. First prepare the dip. Put the coconut and water in a pan and bring slowly to the boil, stirring constantly. Stir in the chilli powder, cumin and coriander, then the garlic and peanut butter.
2. Cook, without boiling, for 5 minutes, stirring constantly. Remove from the heat and stir in the spring onions, soy sauce, and salt and pepper. Leave to cool.
3. If the dip seems too thick, stir in a little cold water. Spoon into a serving bowl and place on a large plate.
4. Cut the pineapple and watermelon into pieces.
5. Arrange the fruits and vegetables around the dip and serve immediately, as an appetizer.

MARINATED FRESH GOAT'S CHEESE

This delicious starter is perfect for a barbecue, as it can be prepared well ahead. Any type of goat's cheese may be used, preferably a fairly plain variety, but it is important that it should be very fresh.

300 g (10 oz) fresh goat's cheese, sliced
2 tablespoons chopped thyme
1 French stick
125 g (4 oz) Herb Butter*
FOR THE DRESSING:
6 tablespoons virgin olive oil
3 tablespoons lemon or lime juice

bouquet garni, to include parsley, thyme and chives
1 tablespoon coarse-grain mustard
1 teaspoon clear honey
2 cloves garlic, crushed
salt and pepper to taste
TO GARNISH:
thyme sprigs

Serves 4–6
Preparation time:
20–25 minutes, plus chilling time
Cooking time:
15–20 minutes
Freezing:
Not recommended

1. Mix the dressing ingredients together.
2. Arrange the cheese in a large dish in a single layer. Pour over the dressing, sprinkle with the thyme and chill for 2 hours.
3. Meanwhile, cut the bread into 1 cm (½ inch) slices, without cutting through the bottom crust. Spread the cut surfaces of the bread with the butter and wrap lightly in foil.
4. Place in a preheated oven, 200°C/400°F/Gas Mark 6, for 15–20 minutes, until crisp and hot. Place in a basket.
5. Garnish the cheese with thyme and serve with the crusty herb bread.

ASPARAGUS IN CREAM SAUCE

Canned asparagus is not suitable for this tasty starter, but at a pinch you could use frozen asparagus. Warm the asparagus and prawn mixture through just before serving.

250 g (8 oz) fresh asparagus, cut into 2.5 cm (1 inch) pieces
15 g (½ oz) butter
1 shallot, chopped very finely
142 ml (5 fl oz) carton double cream

175 g (6 oz) peeled prawns
50 g (2 oz) frozen puff pastry, thawed
salt and pepper to taste
beaten egg or milk to glaze
parsley sprigs to garnish

1. Cook the asparagus in boiling water for 5 minutes; drain, reserving the cooking liquid. Measure the liquid into a jug and reserve 250 ml (8 fl oz).
2. Melt the butter in a pan, add the shallot and cook for 5 minutes, without browning.
3. Add the reserved liquid, bring to the boil and boil rapidly until about 3 tablespoons remain.
4. Add the cream to the pan and boil rapidly for 3 minutes, until thickened. Stir in the asparagus and prawns, and season well with salt and pepper. Cover and set aside.
5. Roll out the pastry on a floured board to about 5 mm (¼ inch) thickness. Using a crescent-shaped or other small cutter, stamp out shapes.
6. Place the pastry shapes on a wetted baking sheet, brush with beaten egg or milk and bake in a preheated oven, 200°C/400°F/Gas Mark 6, for 3–4 minutes, until well risen and golden.
7. Warm the asparagus gently and spoon onto a serving dish or individual plates. Garnish with the pastry crescents and parsley. Serve immediately.

Serves 4
Preparation time: 10–15 minutes
Cooking time: 20 minutes
Freezing: Not recommended

TROUT STUFFED WITH PARMA HAM

4 rainbow trout, gutted but heads and tails left on	*TO GARNISH: lemon or lime wedges or slices*
8 slices Parma ham	*dill sprigs*
*125 g (4 oz) Herb Butter**	

Serves 4
Preparation time: 15 minutes, plus preparing butter
Cooking time: About 15 minutes
Freezing: Not recommended

1. Make diagonal slits in each side of each fish.
2. Roll up the Parma ham and place 2 pieces inside the belly of each trout.
3. Place each trout on a large piece of foil, divide the butter between them and spread over the surface.
4. Wrap the fish in the foil to make parcels, ensuring that there are no gaps for the butter to escape through.
5. Place the fish parcels on the metal grid and cook for 4–5 minutes on each side.
6. Remove the parcels from the barbecue. Carefully lift the fish onto the metal grid, brush liberally with the butter and cook for 2–3 minutes on each side, basting constantly, until the trout are cooked.
7. Lift onto a warmed serving plate and garnish with lemon or lime and dill to serve.

SEAFOOD KEBABS

6 rashers streaky bacon, derinded	*1 quantity Seafood Sauce* to serve*
350 g (12 oz) sole fillets, skinned and cut into 2.5 cm (1 inch) pieces	*FOR THE BASTING SAUCE: grated rind and juice of 1 lemon*
12 cooked prawns in shells	*150 ml (¼ pint) olive oil*
6 scallops, halved if large	*1 bay leaf*
18 bay leaves	*1 parsley sprig*
12 small lemon wedges	*1 thyme sprig*
1 rosemary sprig (optional)	

Serves 6
Preparation time: About 20 minutes, plus making sauce
Cooking time: 10 minutes
Freezing: Not recommended

1. Stretch the bacon rashers with the back of a knife, cut in half and wrap around the pieces of sole.
2. Arrange all the fish alternately on 6 skewers, interspersing with the bay leaves and lemon wedges.
3. Combine the basting ingredients and brush over the kebabs with the rosemary sprig or a basting brush.
4. Place the kebabs on the metal grid and cook for 5 minutes on each side, basting frequently.
5. Serve immediately, with seafood sauce.

SARDINES WITH LEMON BALM BUTTER

12 fresh sardines
olive oil
125 g (4 oz) Lemon Balm
* Butter**

lemon slices or wedges and
* parsley sprigs to garnish*

1. Brush the sardines with olive oil. Place on a fish rack, or directly on the metal grid, and cook for 5 minutes on each side, until tender.

2. Cut the butter into 12 pieces. Place the sardines on a warmed serving plate and top each one with a pat of butter.

3. Garnish with lemon slices or wedges and parsley sprigs. Serve with crusty French bread.

Serves 4–6
Preparation time:
10 minutes, plus preparing butter
Cooking time:
10 minutes
Freezing:
Not recommended

SAUSAGE AND CHICKEN KEBABS

If you cannot buy Italian sausages use other spicy sausages
or, better still, make your own (see page 48).

1 quantity Lime Marinade*
750 g (1½ lb) boneless
  chicken breast, skinned
  and cut into 2.5 cm
  (1 inch) cubes
3 Italian sausages

4 slices French bread,
  2.5 cm (1 inch) thick
several sage and bay leaves
TO GARNISH:
lemon wedges
sage and bay leaves

Serves 6
Preparation time:
25 minutes, plus
making marinade
and marinating
Cooking time:
20 minutes
Freezing:
Not recommended

1. Place the marinade and chicken in a bowl, cover and
chill for 2 hours.
2. Remove the chicken with a slotted spoon, reserving the
marinade.
3. Cut each sausage into 4 pieces.
4. Brush the slices of bread all over with oil and cut into
quarters.
5. Thread the chicken, sausages and bread onto 6 kebab
skewers, interspersing with sage and bay leaves. Place on
the metal grid and cook for 10 minutes on each side,
basting frequently.
6. Garnish with lemon, sage and bay leaves to serve.

CHICKEN SATÉ

*1 quantity Barbecue or
  Lime Marinade**
*750 g (1¹/₂ lb) boneless
  chicken breast, skinned
  and cut into 2.5 cm
  (1 inch) pieces*

*TO SERVE:
coriander leaves
lime or lemon wedges
1 quantity Saté Sauce**

1. Place the marinade and chicken in a large bowl and stir well to coat the chicken. Cover and chill overnight or for 6–8 hours, stirring occasionally.
2. Thread the chicken onto 6 skewers. Place on the metal grid and cook for 5–10 minutes, basting and turning frequently.
3. Garnish with coriander and lime or lemon, and serve with saté sauce.

Serves 6
Preparation time:
10 minutes, plus
making marinade
and sauce, and
marinating
Cooking time:
5–10 minutes
Freezing:
Not recommended

HERBY HOMEMADE SAUSAGES

It is great fun making sausages, and particularly enjoyed by children. Many butchers who make their own sausages will let you have the casings – soak them overnight in cold water and drain before use. It is essential to use very fresh meat in this recipe.

350 g (12 oz) lean pork, minced
250 g (8 oz) belly pork, minced
25 g (1 oz) pork fat, minced
1 small onion, minced
½ teaspoon ground mace
½ teaspoon ground allspice

2 tablespoons each chopped sage, thyme and parsley
dash of Worcestershire sauce
salt and pepper to taste
about 1 metre (3 ft) sausage casing

Makes 10–12
Preparation time: 45 minutes
Cooking time: 20 minutes
Freezing: Recommended for 1 month

1. Mix together all the ingredients in a large bowl, then spoon the sausagemeat into a piping bag fitted with a large plain nozzle.
2. Place the end of the sausage casing over the nozzle and carefully force the sausage mixture into the casing.
3. Push the mixture evenly along the casing, then twist to form sausages and cut.
4. Cook on the metal grid for 20 minutes, turning frequently, until thoroughly cooked and brown.
5. Serve with a selection of mustards and Tomato Sauce* or relishes, and crusty bread.

LAMB CUTLETS WITH MUSTARD SAUCE

In this recipe the cutlets are cooked in a heavy-based frying pan over the coals, so this is a good choice if you are doubtful about the weather, as the food may be cooked indoors.

8 lamb cutlets
4 tablespoons coarse-grain mustard
150 ml (¼ pint) dry white wine
1 tablespoon each chopped thyme, marjoram and oregano

142 ml (5 fl oz) carton double cream
salt and pepper to taste
radicchio leaves and herb sprigs to garnish

1. Place the cutlets in a single layer in a large shallow dish.
2. Place the mustard in a bowl and gradually mix in the wine. Season well with salt and pepper and stir in the herbs.
3. Spoon the marinade over the cutlets, turning them to coat well. Cover and chill for 2 hours.
4. Lift the cutlets from the marinade; reserve the marinade.
5. Heat a heavy-based frying pan over the coals, add the cutlets and brown quickly on both sides, then cook for 1–2 minutes on each side. Pour in the marinade, place the pan over the hottest part of the barbecue and cook rapidly until the lamb is tender and the marinade has reduced to about 3 tablespoons. Transfer the cutlets to a warmed serving dish.
6. Pour the cream into the pan and boil rapidly until the sauce has thickened. Spoon over the cutlets, garnish with radicchio and herbs. Serve immediately.

Serves 4
Preparation time:
10 minutes, plus marinating
Cooking time:
15–20 minutes
Freezing:
Not recommended

POTATO AND CHIVE SALAD

Serves 6
Preparation time:
10 minutes, plus
making dressing
and boiling
potatoes
Freezing:
Not recommended

*1 green chilli, seeded and
   chopped
3 tablespoons snipped
   chives
1 quantity Creamy Herb
   Dressing**

*750 g (1½ lb) tiny new
   potatoes, boiled
bunch of chives, tied
   together, to garnish*

1. Add the chilli and chives to the dressing and mix well to combine. Fold in the potatoes.
2. Transfer to a serving dish and garnish with the chives.

ORANGE AND CUCUMBER SALAD

Serves 4–6
Preparation time:
15–20 minutes,
plus making
dressing
Freezing:
Not recommended

*6 oranges, peeled and cut
   into segments
1 cucumber, sliced thinly*

*150 ml (¼ pint) Orange
   and Mint Dressing*
mint sprigs to garnish*

1. Arrange the oranges and cucumbers in concentric circles on 1 large or 4 small flat serving plates.
2. Spoon over the dressing and garnish with mint sprigs to serve.

ENDIVE AND ROQUEFORT SALAD

*4 slices white bread
4 tablespoons oil for frying
1 curly endive or frisé
2 heads radicchio
125 g (4 oz) Roquefort
   cheese, crumbled
125 ml (4 fl oz) French
   Dressing**

*FOR THE GARLIC
   MAYONNAISE:
2 tablespoons
   Mayonnaise*
1 small clove garlic,
   crushed
1 teaspoon chopped basil
salt and pepper to taste*

Serves 4–6
Preparation time:
About 20 minutes,
plus making
dressing
Freezing:
Not recommended

Illustrated top
right: Honeysuckle
Cup (page 72)

1. First, combine all the ingredients for the garlic mayonnaise.
2. Cut the bread into heart shapes, using a metal cutter. Heat the oil in a pan, add the bread and fry until golden brown. Drain on kitchen paper.
3. Tear the endive into pieces and separate the radicchio into leaves. Place in a bowl. Stir in the cheese and dressing. Spoon onto a serving plate.
4. Spread the croûtons with the mayonnaise and arrange around the edge of the salad. Serve immediately.

RICE AND ARTICHOKE SALAD

It is essential not to overcook the rice—it should be *al dente* (firm to the tooth, in literal translation). The flavour improves if the salad is dressed about 1 hour before serving.

*125 g (4 oz) long-grain
    rice
150 ml (¹/4 pint) Herb and
    Peppercorn Dressing*
4 tomatoes, skinned,
    seeded and chopped
50 g (2 oz) button
    mushrooms, halved if
    large*

*400 g (14 oz) can
    artichoke hearts,
    drained and quartered
50 g (2 oz) black olives
3 spring onions, chopped
salt to taste
2 tablespoons chopped
    basil or parsley to
    garnish*

Serves 4–6
Preparation time:
20 minutes, plus
making dressing
and standing time
Cooking time:
12–14 minutes
Freezing:
Not recommended

1. Cook the rice in boiling salted water for 12–14 minutes, until *al dente*: drain and rinse under running cold water. Drain well.
2. Place the rice in a large bowl, add the herb dressing, tomatoes, mushrooms, artichokes, black olives and spring onions; toss thoroughly.
3. Pile the rice salad into a serving bowl and leave to stand for 1 hour.
4. Sprinkle with the basil or parsley to serve.

BEAN SALAD

The combination of beans and tuna is very good. In this case, the tuna is in the dressing, giving a rich creaminess to the beans. The dressing also makes a nice change on a green or mixed salad.

*432 g (15¹/4 oz) can red
    kidney beans, drained
400 g (14 oz) can white
    kidney beans, drained
410 g (14¹/2 oz) can
    flageolets, drained
2 shallots, chopped finely
3 celery sticks, sliced
125 g (4 oz) button
    mushrooms, sliced
1 curly endive or
    frisé*

*FOR THE DRESSING:
150 ml (¹/4 pint)
    Mayonnaise*
1 tablespoon lemon juice
99 g (3¹/2 oz) can tuna,
    drained and flaked
4 parsley sprigs
dash of Tabasco
1 clove garlic, sliced
2 tablespoons snipped
    chives
salt and pepper to taste*

1. First, make the dressing. Place the mayonnaise, lemon juice, tuna, parsley, Tabasco and garlic in a food processor or blender and work until smooth. Stir in the chives, and salt and pepper.

2. Place all the beans in a colander and wash thoroughly under running cold water; drain well.

3. Mix together the beans, shallots, celery and mushrooms. Fold in the dressing.

4. Arrange the endive on a flat serving plate and pile the beans in the centre.

Serves 6–8
Preparation time:
25 minutes
Freezing:
Not recommended

SALAD WITH ALMOND DRESSING

1/4 iceberg lettuce
1/4 curly endive or frisé
1/4 cucumber, sliced
125 g (4 oz) spinach leaves
1 green pepper, cored,
seeded and sliced
1 bunch watercress
50 g (2 oz) nasturtium
flowers

1 avocado, peeled, stoned,
sliced and sprinkled with
lemon juice
1 carton mustard and
cress
175 ml (6 fl oz) Almond
Dressing*
25 g (1 oz) flaked
almonds, toasted

Serves 6
Preparation time:
20 minutes, plus
making dressing
Freezing:
Not recommended

1. Tear the lettuce and endive into pieces and place in a bowl with the cucumber.
2. Tear the spinach into pieces and add to the bowl with the green pepper, watercress and nasturtiums. Add the avocado and mustard and cress and toss the salad well.
3. Fold the dressing into the salad and sprinkle with the almonds just before serving.

RATATOUILLE WITH CORIANDER

Ratatouille is a good accompaniment to barbecued meat and fish. It also makes a delicious starter.

1 aubergine, sliced
2 tablespoons olive oil
2 onions, sliced
397 g (14 oz) can chopped
tomatoes
2 tablespoons white wine
2 cloves garlic, crushed
2 courgettes, sliced

1 green pepper, cored,
seeded and sliced
1 yellow or red pepper,
cored, seeded and sliced
salt and pepper to taste
2 tablespoons chopped
coriander (optional)
coriander leaves to garnish
(optional)

Serves 4
Preparation time:
30 minutes
Cooking time:
35–40 minutes
Freezing:
Recommended

1. Layer the aubergine slices in a colander and sprinkle liberally with salt. Leave to drain for 30 minutes, then rinse thoroughly under running cold water. Leave to drain.
2. Heat the oil in a large pan, add the onion and fry for 5 minutes, without browning.
3. Stir in the tomatoes, wine and garlic.
4. Add the courgettes, aubergine, peppers, and salt and pepper.
5. Cover and simmer for 35–40 minutes, until the vegetables are soft. Stir in the coriander, if using. Serve warm, garnished with coriander, if you wish.

BARBECUED CORN ON THE COB

6 corn cobs
175 g (6 oz) butter,
softened

1 tablespoon each chopped
parsley, chives, tarragon
and thyme
pepper to taste

1. Cook the corn cobs in boiling water for 7 minutes. Drain and place each cob on a large piece of foil.
2. Cream the butter until soft, then stir in the herbs.
3. Divide the butter between the corn, spreading evenly over the top. Sprinkle with pepper.
4. Seal the foil into parcels, ensuring that there is no gap for the butter to escape through.
5. Cook over the coals of the barbecue for 20–25 minutes, until tender. Serve immediately.

Serves 6
Preparation time:
10 minutes
Cooking time:
20–25 minutes
Freezing:
Not recommended

OLD-FASHIONED GOOSEBERRY FOOL

500 g (1 lb) gooseberries
3 tablespoons icing sugar,
or to taste
284 ml (10 fl oz) carton
double cream

green food colouring
(optional)
mint sprigs to decorate

Serves 4
Preparation time:
20 minutes
Cooking time:
15 minutes
Freezing:
Not recommended

1. Place the gooseberries in a saucepan, cover and cook over a very low heat for 15 minutes, until the fruit is very soft, shaking the pan occasionally.
2. Remove from the heat. Stir in the icing sugar, taste and add more if you wish. Leave to cool.
3. Rub the gooseberries through a nylon sieve.
4. Whip the cream until it stands in peaks, then fold in the purée and a little green colouring, if using.
5. Spoon into 4 glass dishes and chill until required. Serve decorated with mint sprigs.

REDCURRANT AND KIWI PAVLOVAS

2 egg whites
pinch of salt
125 g (4 oz) caster sugar
¼ teaspoon almond
essence
¼ teaspoon vinegar
2 teaspoons cold water
175 g (6 oz) redcurrants

50 g (2 oz) granulated
sugar or to taste
2–3 tablespoons
maraschino liqueur
284 ml (10 fl oz) carton
whipping cream
2 kiwi fruit, sliced and
quartered

Serves 6
Preparation time:
30 minutes, plus cooling
Cooking time:
1 hour
Freezing:
Not recommended

1. Whisk the egg whites and salt until very stiff. Gradually whisk in the caster sugar, then whisk in the almond essence, vinegar and water.
2. Spoon the mixture into 6 small rounds on a baking sheet lined with baking parchment. Flatten the centres.
3. Bake in a preheated oven, 140°C/275°F/Gas Mark 1, for 1 hour. Turn off the heat and leave the meringues in the oven until it is cold.
4. Place the redcurrants in a pan, cover and cook over a low heat for 2 minutes, shaking the pan occasionally.
5. Remove from the heat, stir in granulated sugar and liqueur to taste and leave until cold.
6. Whip the cream until it forms peaks, then fold in the redcurrants and their juice.
7. Lift the pavlovas onto a serving plate. Fill each with the cream and top with the kiwi slices. Serve immediately.

Illustrated top:
Strawberry
Champagne Punch
(page 72)

RASPBERRY SORBET IN BASKETS

These look very impressive but are so simple to make. I like the flavour and texture of raspberry sorbet with the baskets, but any sorbet or ice cream may be used. Store any remaining baskets in an airtight tin for up to 1 week.

RASPBERRY SORBET:
1 tablespoon clear honey
300 ml (½ pint) red grape juice
625 g (1¼ lb) raspberries
juice of ½ lemon
1 egg white
BRANDY SNAP BASKETS:
25 g (1 oz) plain flour
¼ teaspoon ground ginger
25 g (1 oz) unsalted butter, softened

65 g (2½ oz) caster sugar
25 g (1 oz) golden syrup
TO SERVE:
125 g (4 oz) raspberries
142 ml (5 fl oz) carton whipping cream, whipped
raspberry or mint leaves to decorate (optional)

Serves 6
Preparation time:
40 minutes, plus chilling
Cooking:
About 25 minutes
Freezing:
Not recommended

1. Stir the honey into the grape juice.
2. Rub the raspberries through a nylon sieve. Place the purée in a bowl and stir in the grape juice and lemon juice.
3. Pour into a rigid freezerproof container, cover, seal and freeze for about 2 hours or until mushy. Beat thoroughly.
4. Whisk the egg white until very stiff, then fold into the raspberry mixture. Cover, seal and freeze until firm.
5. Meanwhile, make the baskets. Line 3 baking sheets with baking parchment.
6. Sift the flour and ginger together and set aside.
7. Cream the butter and sugar together until light and fluffy, then beat in the syrup. Stir in the flour and mix to a dough.
8. Turn onto a working surface and knead until smooth. Chill for 1 hour.
9. Place 2 spoonfuls of the mixture well apart on each prepared baking sheet and flatten slightly with the hand.
10. Place one baking sheet at a time in a preheated oven, 190°C/375°F/Gas Mark 5, and cook for 8 minutes, until the brandy snaps are golden.
11. Leave to cool for a few minutes, then lift each brandy snap off the paper and mould it over an orange. Leave to cool, then lift off and arrange on a serving plate.
12. Spoon or scoop the sorbet into each basket and serve with raspberries and whipped cream. Decorate with raspberry or mint leaves if you wish.

SUMMER FRUIT COMPOTE

750 g (1½ lb) soft fruit, e.g.
raspberries, redcurrants,
blackcurrants,
blackberries

125 g (4 oz) caster sugar,
or to taste
6 petit-suisses
few raspberry or mint
leaves to decorate

1. Place the prepared fruit in a pan, cover and cook very gently for 15 minutes, shaking the pan occasionally.
2. Remove from the heat and add the sugar. Cool, then chill for 1 hour. Place the petit-suisses in the freezer for 1 hour.
3. Cut each frozen petit-suisse in half.
4. Spoon the fruit into 6 individual dishes, arrange the petit suisse slices on one side and decorate with raspberry or mint leaves.

Serves 6
Preparation time:
20 minutes, plus chilling and freezing
Cooking time:
15 minutes
Freezing:
Recommended for fruit compote only

PATIO MEALS

There is something very special about eating outside, especially on a balmy summer evening with the scent of flowers in the air.

Give particular thought to the table arrangement. Arrange fresh flowers in tiny vases at each place setting, or place small candles on the table.

Instead of using grapes for the cheeseboard, garnish it with fresh figs, sliced watermelon and pineapple, or clusters of fresh herbs or flowers.

MENU 1	MENU 2
Serves 6	Serves 4
Melon and Orange Salad	Iced Watercress Soup
Paella	Salmon with Herby Hollandaise
Spanish Pepper Salad	New Potatoes in Basil Butter
Raspberry Crème Brûlée	Chilled Fresh Asparagus
Cheeseboard	Mixed Green Salad
Crisp Apples	Strawberry Fools
	Cheeseboard
Wines: Sangria (see page 73) as an aperitif, Spanish Cava, Rioja	Wines: Italian Tocai, Graves or sparkling Vouvray

MELON AND ORANGE SALAD

This is a light, clean-tasting starter to act as an appetizer before the Paella.

1 large ogen or galia melon
4 oranges

8 kumquats, sliced thinly
4–6 tablespoons Cointreau
mint sprigs to decorate

Serves 6
Preparation time:
30 minutes, plus chilling
Freezing:
Not recommended

1. Cut the melon in half and scoop out the flesh with a melon baller, or cut into cubes. Place in a bowl, adding any juice.
2. Thinly pare the rind from 1 orange and cut into narrow strips. Place in a small saucepan, cover with boiling water, bring to the boil, then simmer for 5 minutes. Drain and cool, then add to the melon.
3. Peel the oranges, cutting away all the pith and membrane. Cut into segments and add to the melon.

Illustrated top right: Sangria (page 73)

4. Stir the kumquats into the other fruit, pour over the Cointreau and mix well. Cover and chill for 1 hour.
5. Serve in individual dishes, decorated with mint.

SPANISH PEPPER SALAD

By grilling the peppers in this way, the skin peels away very
easily and leaves the flesh slightly soft. It will then absorb
the flavour of the dressing more readily.

2 green peppers
2 red peppers
2 yellow peppers
*1 tablespoon each chopped
    oregano and thyme*

*150 ml (¹/₄ pint) French
    Dressing**
thyme sprigs to garnish

Serves 6
Preparation time:
20 minutes
Freezing:
Not recommended

1. Place the peppers under a preheated hot grill until the
skins are charred, turning frequently. Leave to cool, then
peel away the skin. Remove the cores and seeds and slice
the flesh. Arrange on a serving plate.
2. Add the herbs to the dressing and shake well to blend.
Spoon the dressing over the peppers and garnish with
thyme sprigs. Serve as an accompaniment to the Paella.

PAELLA

An ideal outdoor dish with a Spanish flavour.

*1 chicken, weighing 1.5 kg
    (3 lb)*
7 cloves garlic
*1 bouquet garni, to
    include bay leaf,
    rosemary, parsley and
    thyme*
1 litre (1³/₄ pints) water
12 fresh mussels, scrubbed
12 fresh clams (optional)
*2 cleaned squid, sliced
    crossways*
4 tablespoons olive oil
2 onions, chopped
*500 g (1 lb) Italian risotto
    rice*

*¹/₂ teaspoon saffron
    threads, infused in a
    little boiling water*
*1 each red and green
    pepper, cored, seeded
    and sliced*
250 g (8 oz) peeled prawns
*6 Dublin Bay prawns
    (optional)*
125 g (4 oz) shelled peas
salt and pepper to taste
TO GARNISH:
whole prawns
lemon wedges
chopped parsley

1. Cut the chicken into 6 pieces. Remove the wing tips and
place in a large saucepan. Set the chicken aside.
2. Add the chicken trimmings, 4 cloves garlic, the bouquet
garni, water, and salt and pepper to the pan, bring to the
boil, cover and simmer for 30 minutes. Strain and reserve.

3. Meanwhile, cook the mussels, discarding any that have already opened, clams if using, and squid in a little boiling salted water for 3 minutes, until the shellfish open. Discard any that do not open. Drain and set aside.

4. Heat the oil in a very large frying pan, add the chicken pieces and brown quickly. Remove from the pan and set aside.

5. Crush the remaining garlic, add to the pan with the onion and cook for 5–10 minutes, until lightly browned.

6. Return the chicken to the pan. Add the rice, reserved chicken stock, saffron threads with their liquid, and salt. Stir in the peppers, bring to the boil and cook rapidly for 5 minutes, stirring occasionally.

7. Add the mussels, clams if using, squid, prawns and peas. Lower the heat and cook for 10 minutes, until the rice and chicken are tender and the fish hot.

8. Leave to stand for 5 minutes, stirring occasionally, then garnish with prawns and lemon wedges. Sprinkle with chopped parsley and serve immediately.

Serves 6
Preparation time:
35–40 minutes
Cooking time:
About 25 minutes
Freezing:
Not recommended

ORANGE AND GINGER SAUCE

Serve with pork and lamb chops, and kebabs.

**Makes 250 ml
(8 fl oz)
Preparation time:**
5–10 minutes
Freezing:
Not recommended

*6 pieces stem ginger in
    syrup, sliced
6 tablespoons of the ginger
    syrup
1 clove garlic, crushed*

*grated rind and juice of
    2 large oranges
pinch of dried mixed herbs
salt and pepper to taste*

Mix all the ingredients together and use as required.

SEAFOOD SAUCE

Serve with any white, but not oily, fish.

**Makes about
200 ml (⅓ pint)
Preparation time:**
10 minutes
Freezing:
Not recommended

*6 tablespoons
    Mayonnaise*
2 tomatoes, skinned,
    seeded and diced
1 tablespoon lemon juice
½ teaspoon Worcestershire
    sauce*

*1 clove garlic, crushed
1 tablespoon chopped
    parsley
1 teaspoon finely grated
    lemon rind
salt and pepper to taste*

Mix all the ingredients together in a bowl, cover and chill
for 20 minutes. Use as required.

SATÉ SAUCE

This makes an unusual but delicious accompaniment to
barbecued pork and lamb cutlets.

**Makes about
300 ml (½ pint)
Preparation time:**
5 minutes
Cooking time:
7 minutes
Freezing:
Not recommended

*100 g (3½ oz) creamed
    coconut
150 ml (¼ pint) water
1–2 cloves garlic, crushed
2.5 cm (1 inch) piece fresh
    root ginger, crushed*

*½–1 teaspoon chilli
    powder
1 teaspoon ground cumin
1 teaspoon ground
    coriander
125 g (4 oz) crunchy
    peanut butter*

1. Place the coconut in a pan, stir in the water, then cook
over a low heat, stirring, until dissolved and creamy.
2. Stir in the garlic, ginger and spices and cook for
5 minutes, stirring occasionally. Stir in the peanut butter
and cook for 2 minutes. Serve hot or cold.

TOMATO SAUCE

2 tablespoons oil
4 shallots, chopped finely
3 cloves garlic, crushed
539 g (1 lb 3 oz) can
   peeled tomatoes

300 ml (½ pint) dry white
   wine
2 tablespoons each
   chopped parsley, basil
   and thyme
salt and pepper to taste

1. Heat the oil in a large pan, add the shallots and cook for 5 minutes, without browning.
2. Stir in the garlic, tomatoes with their juice, wine and herbs. Season with salt and pepper.
3. Bring to the boil, then simmer, uncovered, for 30 minutes, stirring occasionally to break up the tomatoes.
4. Increase heat and boil rapidly for 5–10 minutes, until the sauce has reduced and thickened. Serve hot or cold.

Makes about
450 ml (¾ pint)
Preparation time:
10 minutes
Cooking time:
about 40 minutes
Freezing:
Recommended

FLAVOURED BUTTERS

Flavoured butters are a good standby for impromptu barbecues. They add flavour and moisture to meat and fish, and turn a plainly cooked steak into something special. Lemon Butter is excellent with poultry; Blue Cheese Butter is great with steaks and beefburgers.

175 g (6 oz) butter,
   softened
GARLIC BUTTER:
3 cloves garlic, crushed
2 tablespoons chopped
   parsley
LEMON BUTTER:
3 tablespoons lemon juice
2 teaspoons finely grated
   lemon rind
BLUE CHEESE BUTTER:
125 g (4 oz) Danish blue
   cheese, creamed
pinch of cayenne pepper

HERB BUTTER:
1 tablespoon each chopped
   parsley, chives, thyme
   and tarragon
1 teaspoon lemon juice
LEMON BALM OR THYME
   BUTTER:
2 cloves garlic, crushed
2 tablespoons lemon juice
2 teaspoons finely grated
   lemon rind
3 tablespoons chopped
   lemon balm or thyme
salt and pepper to taste

1. Place the butter in a bowl and beat until soft. Beat in the chosen flavouring ingredients.
2. Place the butter on a piece of foil and form into a roll. Wrap in the foil and chill for 1 hour.
3. Slice and use as required.

Serves 4
Preparation time:
5–10 minutes
Freezing:
Recommended

SALAD DRESSINGS

MAYONNAISE

Homemade mayonnaise has a delicious flavour and takes very little time to prepare. It can be stored in an airtight contained in the refrigerator for up to 10 days.

2 egg yolks
pinch of dry mustard
2 tablespoons wine
* vinegar*
150 ml (¼ pint) olive oil

150 ml (¼ pint) sunflower
* oil*
1 tablespoon boiling water
salt and pepper to taste

Makes about
300 ml (½ pint)
Preparation time:
10 minutes
Freezing:
Not recommended

1. Place the egg yolks, mustard and wine vinegar in a blender or food processor. Add a little salt and, using the slowest speed, blend together.
2. With the machine running, gradually pour in the oil. Once it has started to thicken, add the oil more quickly in a steady stream.
3. Add the boiling water and blend for a few seconds. Use as required.

FRENCH DRESSING

Virgin olive oil, which is green in colour, is superior in flavour to ordinary olive oil and improves dressings enormously. Use 1 or 2 cloves garlic, according to personal taste. Any left-over dressing can be stored in the refrigerator for up to 2 weeks.

125 ml (4 fl oz) olive oil
4 tablespoons lemon juice
1½ teaspoons coarse-
* grain mustard*

1½ teaspoons clear honey
1–2 cloves garlic, crushed
salt and pepper to taste

Makes 175 ml
(6 fl oz)
Preparation time:
5 minutes
Freezing:
Not recommended

Place the ingredients in a screw-topped jar and shake well to blend. Use as required.

VARIATIONS
Soy Sauce Dressing: Replace the lemon juice with soy sauce. Omit the honey and mustard, and add 2.5 cm (1 inch) piece crushed fresh root ginger. A tasty dressing, ideal for rice and bean sprout salads.

Herb and Peppercorn Dressing: Add 2 teaspoons each chopped parsley, thyme and chives, and 1 tablespoon green peppercorns. Use with leafy green salads, mushroom salads, and tomato salads.

Orange and Mint Dressing: Replace the lemon juice with fresh orange juice. Add 1 teaspoon wine vinegar, 2 tablespoons chopped mint and 1 tablespoon chopped marjoram. A nice refreshing dressing—and a perfect complement for chicory, cucumber and watercress salads.

CREAMY HERB DRESSING

If you are concerned with fat content or calories, use the 0% fat fromage frais rather than the 40% fat. If you prefer, use soured cream instead of fromage frais.

5 tablespoons natural fromage frais	*1 tablespoon each chopped parsley and thyme*
5 tablespoons natural yogurt	*1 clove garlic, crushed (optional)*
2 spring onions, chopped very finely	*dash of Tabasco salt and pepper to taste*

Mix all the ingredients together in a small bowl and use as required.

Makes 175 ml (6 fl oz) Preparation: 10 minutes **Freezing:** Not recommended

VARIATIONS

Blue Cheese Dressing: Omit the garlic and thyme. Mash 50 g (2 oz) blue Stilton cheese in a bowl with 2–3 tablespoons milk until smooth. Stir in the remaining ingredients.

Almond Dressing: Omit the parsley, thyme and Tabasco. Add 50 g (2 oz) ground almonds, and the grated rind and juice of 1 lime. Stir in 2–3 tablespoons single cream, to give a thinner consistency.

INDEX

Photography by: James Jackson
Designed by: Sue Storey
Home economists: Clare Gordon-Smith & Carole Handslip
Stylist: Maggie Heinz
Jacket photograph by: Paul Williams
Illustration by: Linda Smith
Typeset by Rowland Phototypesetting Ltd